This
Knitting Planner
belongs to:

. . . .

Index

Project: Page:

_____   _____

_____   _____

_____   _____

_____   _____

_____   _____

_____   _____

_____   _____

_____   _____

_____   _____

_____   _____

_____   _____

_____   _____

_____   _____

_____   _____

_____   _____

_____   _____

_____   _____

_____   _____

_____   _____

_____   _____

_____   _____

_____   _____

Index

Project:

Page:

Index

Project: Page:

_____   _____

_____   _____

_____   _____

_____   _____

_____   _____

_____   _____

_____   _____

_____   _____

_____   _____

_____   _____

_____   _____

_____   _____

_____   _____

_____   _____

_____   _____

_____   _____

_____   _____

_____   _____

_____   _____

_____   _____

_____   _____

_____   _____

_____   _____

I Am Knitting ....

And I am making it for: ....

I started: .... And I finished: ....

Needles:		
Size	Type	Length

paste yarn samples here!

Yarns:	Dye lot:	No. of Skeins

Notes:

_____

_____

_____

_____

_____

_____

_____

I Am Knitting ....

And I am making it for: ....

I started: .... And I finished: ....

Needles:		
Size	Type	Length

paste yarn samples here!

Yarns:	Dye lot:	No. of Skeins

Notes:

_____

_____

_____

_____

_____

_____

_____

I Am Knitting ....

And I am making it for: ....

I started: .... And I finished: ....

Needles:		
Size	Type	Length

paste yarn samples here!

Yarns:		Dye lot:	No. of Skeins

Notes: _____

_____

_____

_____

_____

_____

_____

I Am Knitting ....

And I am making it for: ....

I started: .... And I finished: ....

Needles:		
Size	Type	Length

paste yarn samples here!

13

Yarns:	Dye lot:	No. of Skeins

Notes:

_____

_____

_____

_____

_____

_____

_____

I Am Knitting ....

And I am making it for: ....

I started: .... And I finished: ....

Needles:		
Size	Type	Length

paste yarn samples here!

Yarns:	Dye lot:	No. of Skeins

Notes:

_____

_____

_____

_____

_____

_____

_____

I Am Knitting ....

And I am making it for: ....

I started: .... And I finished: ....

Needles:		
Size	Type	Length

paste yarn samples here!

Yarns:	Dye lot:	No. of Skeins

Notes:
_____

_____

_____

_____

_____

_____

I Am Knitting ....

And I am making it for: ....

I started: .... And I finished: ....

Needles:		
Size	Type	Length

paste yarn samples here!

Yarns:	Dye lot:	No. of Skeins

Notes:

_____

_____

_____

_____

_____

_____

I Am Knitting ....

And I am making it for: ....

I started: .... And I finished: ....

Needles:		
Size	Type	Length

paste yarn samples here!

Yarns:	Dye lot:	No. of Skeins

Notes:

_____

_____

_____

_____

_____

_____

I Am Knitting ....

And I am making it for: ....

I started: ....   And I finished: ....

Needles:		
Size	Type	Length

paste yarn samples here!

Yarns:		Dye lot:	No. of Skeins

Notes:

_____

_____

_____

_____

_____

_____

_____

I Am Knitting ....

And I am making it for: ....

I started: .... And I finished: ....

Needles:		
Size	Type	Length

paste yarn samples here!

Yarns:	Dye lot:	No. of Skeins

Notes:

_____

_____

_____

_____

_____

_____

I Am Knitting ....

And I am making it for: ....

I started: .... And I finished: ....

Needles:		
Size	Type	Length

paste yarn samples here!

Yarns:	Dye lot:	No. of Skeins

Notes:

_____

_____

_____

_____

_____

_____

_____

I Am Knitting ....

And I am making it for: ....

I started: .... And I finished: ....

Needles:		
Size	Type	Length

paste yarn samples here!

Yarns:	Dye lot:	No. of Skeins

Notes:

_____

_____

_____

_____

_____

_____

_____

I Am Knitting ....

And I am making it for: ....

I started: .... And I finished: ....

Needles:		
Size	Type	Length

paste yarn samples here!

Yarns:	Dye lot:	No. of Skeins

Notes:

_____

_____

_____

_____

_____

_____

_____

I Am Knitting ....

And I am making it for: ....

I started: ....   And I finished: ....

Needles:		
Size	Type	Length

paste yarn samples here!

Yarns:	Dye lot:	No. of Skeins

Notes:

_____

_____

_____

_____

_____

_____

_____

I Am Knitting ....

And I am making it for: ....

I started: .... And I finished: ....

Needles:		
Size	Type	Length

paste yarn samples here!

Yarns:	Dye lot:	No. of Skeins

Notes:

_____

_____

_____

_____

_____

_____

_____

I Am Knitting ....

And I am making it for: ....

I started: ....   And I finished: ....

Needles:		
Size	Type	Length

paste yarn samples here!

Yarns:	Dye lot:	No. of Skeins

Notes:

_____

_____

_____

_____

_____

_____

I Am Knitting ....

And I am making it for: ....

I started: ....   And I finished: ....

Needles:		
Size	Type	Length

paste yarn samples here!

Yarns:	Dye lot:	No. of Skeins

Notes:

_____

_____

_____

_____

_____

_____

_____

I Am Knitting ....

And I am making it for: ....

I started: .... And I finished: ....

Needles:		
Size	Type	Length

paste yarn samples here!

Yarns:		Dye lot:	No. of Skeins

Notes:

_____

_____

_____

_____

_____

_____

_____

I Am Knitting ....

And I am making it for: ....

I started: .... And I finished: ....

Needles:		
Size	Type	Length

paste yarn samples here!

43

Yarns:	Dye lot:	No. of Skeins

Notes:

_____

_____

_____

_____

_____

_____

_____

I Am Knitting ....

And I am making it for: ....

I started: .... And I finished: ....

Needles:		
Size	Type	Length

paste yarn samples here!

Yarns:	Dye lot:	No. of Skeins

Notes:

_____

_____

_____

_____

_____

_____

_____

I Am Knitting ....

And I am making it for: ....

I started: ....   And I finished: ....

Needles:		
Size	Type	Length

paste yarn samples here!

Yarns:		Dye lot:	No. of Skeins

Notes:

_____

_____

_____

_____

_____

_____

I Am Knitting ....

And I am making it for: ....

I started: .... And I finished: ....

Needles:		
Size	Type	Length

paste yarn samples here!

Yarns:	Dye lot:	No. of Skeins

Notes:

_____

_____

_____

_____

_____

_____

_____

I Am Knitting ....

And I am making it for: ....

I started: ....   And I finished: ....

Needles:		
Size	Type	Length

paste yarn samples here!

Yarns:		Dye lot:	No. of Skeins

Notes:

_____

_____

_____

_____

_____

_____

_____

I Am Knitting ....

And I am making it for: ....

I started: .... And I finished: ....

Needles:		
Size	Type	Length

paste yarn samples here!

Yarns:	Dye lot:	No. of Skeins

53

Notes:

_____

_____

_____

_____

_____

_____

_____

I Am Knitting ....

And I am making it for: ....

I started: .... And I finished: ....

Needles:		
Size	Type	Length

paste yarn samples here!

Yarns:	Dye lot:	No. of Skeins

Notes:
_____

_____

_____

_____

_____

_____

_____

I Am Knitting ....

And I am making it for: ....

I started: .... And I finished: ....

Needles:		
Size	Type	Length

paste yarn samples here!

Yarns:	Dye lot:	No. of Skeins

Notes:

_____

_____

_____

_____

_____

_____

_____

I Am Knitting ....

And I am making it for: ....

I started: .... And I finished: ....

Needles:		
Size	Type	Length

paste yarn samples here!

Yarns:	Dye lot:	No. of Skeins

Notes:

_____

_____

_____

_____

_____

_____

I Am Knitting ....

And I am making it for: ....

I started: ....   And I finished: ....

Needles:		
Size	Type	Length

paste yarn samples here!

Yarns:	Dye lot:	No. of Skeins

Notes:

_____

_____

_____

_____

_____

_____

_____

I Am Knitting ....

And I am making it for: ....

I started: .... And I finished: ....

Needles:		
Size	Type	Length

yarn paste samples here!

Yarns:	Dye lot:	No. of Skeins

Notes:

_____

_____

_____

_____

_____

_____

_____

I Am Knitting ....

And I am making it for: ....

I started: .... And I finished: ....

Needles:		
Size	Type	Length

paste yarn samples here!

Yarns:	Dye lot:	No. of Skeins

Notes:

_____

_____

_____

_____

_____

_____

_____

I Am Knitting ....

And I am making it for: ....

I started: .... And I finished: ....

Needles:		
Size	Type	Length

paste yarn samples here!

Yarns:	Dye lot:	No. of Skeins

Notes:
_____
_____
_____
_____
_____
_____
_____

I Am Knitting ....

And I am making it for: ....

I started: .... And I finished: ....

Needles:		
Size	Type	Length

paste yarn samples here!

Yarns:	Dye lot:	No. of Skeins

Notes:

_____

_____

_____

_____

_____

_____

I Am Knitting ....

And I am making it for: ....

I started: .... And I finished: ....

Needles:		
Size	Type	Length

paste yarn samples here!

71

Yarns:	Dye lot:	No. of Skeins

Notes:

_____

_____

_____

_____

_____

_____

_____

I Am Knitting ....

And I am making it for: ....

I started: .... And I finished: ....

Needles:		
Size	Type	Length

paste yarn samples here!

Yarns:	Dye lot:	No. of Skeins

Notes:

_____

_____

_____

_____

_____

_____

_____

I Am Knitting ....

And I am making it for: ....

I started: .... And I finished: ....

Needles:		
Size	Type	Length

paste yarn samples here!

Yarns:	Dye lot:	No. of Skeins

Notes:

_____

_____

_____

_____

_____

_____

_____

I Am Knitting ....

And I am making it for: ....

I started: .... And I finished: ....

Needles:		
Size	Type	Length

paste yarn samples here!

Yarns:	Dye lot:	No. of Skeins

Notes:

_____

_____

_____

_____

_____

_____

_____

I Am Knitting ....

And I am making it for: ....

I started: .... And I finished: ....

Needles:		
Size	Type	Length

paste yarn samples here!

Yarns:	Dye lot:	No. of Skeins

Notes:

_____

_____

_____

_____

_____

_____

I Am Knitting ....

And I am making it for: ....

I started: .... And I finished: ....

Needles:		
Size	Type	Length

paste yarn samples here!

Yarns:	Dye lot:	No. of Skeins

Notes:

_____

_____

_____

_____

_____

_____

_____

I Am Knitting ....

And I am making it for: ....

I started: .... And I finished: ....

Needles:		
Size	Type	Length

paste yarn samples here!

Yarns:	Dye lot:	No. of Skeins

Notes:

_____

_____

_____

_____

_____

_____

_____

I Am Knitting ....

And I am making it for: ....

I started: .... And I finished: ....

Needles:		
Size	Type	Length

paste yarn samples here!

Yarns:	Dye lot:	No. of Skeins

Notes:

_____

_____

_____

_____

_____

_____

_____

I Am Knitting ....

And I am making it for: ....

I started: .... And I finished: ....

Needles:		
Size	Type	Length

paste yarn samples here!

Yarns:		Dye lot:	No. of Skeins

Notes:

_____

_____

_____

_____

_____

_____

_____

I Am Knitting ....

And I am making it for: ....

I started: .... And I finished: ....

Needles:		
Size	Type	Length

paste yarn samples here!

Yarns:		Dye lot:	No.of Skeins

Notes:

_____

_____

_____

_____

_____

_____

_____

I Am Knitting ....

And I am making it for: ....

I started: .... And I finished: ....

Needles:		
Size	Type	Length

paste yarn samples here!

Yarns:	Dye lot:	No. of Skeins

Notes:

_____

_____

_____

_____

_____

_____

_____

I Am Knitting ....

And I am making it for: ....

I started: .... And I finished: ....

Needles:		
Size	Type	Length

paste
yarn samples
here!

Yarns:	Dye lot:	No. of Skeins

Notes:

_____

_____

_____

_____

_____

_____

_____

_____

I Am Knitting ....

And I am making it for: ....

I started: .... And I finished: ....

Needles:		
Size	Type	Length

paste yarn samples here!

Yarns:	Dye lot:	No. of Skeins

Notes:

_____

_____

_____

_____

_____

_____

_____

I Am Knitting ....

And I am making it for: ....

I started: .... And I finished: ....

Needles:		
Size	Type	Length

paste yarn samples here!

Yarns:	Dye lot:	No. of Skeins

Notes:

_____

_____

_____

_____

_____

_____

_____

I Am Knitting ....

And I am making it for: ....

I started: .... And I finished: ....

Needles:		
Size	Type	Length

paste yarn samples here!

Yarns:	Dye lot:	No. of Skeins

Notes:

_____

_____

_____

_____

_____

_____

_____

I Am Knitting ....

And I am making it for: ....

I started: .... And I finished: ....

Needles:		
Size	Type	Length

paste yarn samples here!

Yarns:		Dye lot:	No. of Skeins

Notes:

_____

_____

_____

_____

_____

_____

_____

I Am Knitting ....

And I am making it for: ....

I started: .... And I finished: ....

Needles:		
Size	Type	Length

paste yarn samples here!

Yarns:	Dye lot:	No. of Skeins

Notes:

_____

_____

_____

_____

_____

_____

_____

I Am Knitting ....

And I am making it for: ....

I started: .... And I finished: ....

Needles:		
Size	Type	Length

paste yarn samples here!

Yarns:	Dye lot:	No. of Skeins

Notes:

_____

_____

_____

_____

_____

_____

_____

Yarn Inventory

Name:	Dye lot:	Source:	No. of Skeins

Yarn Inventory

Name:	Dye lot:	Source:	No. of Skeins

Yarn Inventory

Name:	Dye lot:	Source:	No. of Skeins

Yarn Inventory

Name:	Dye lot:	Source:	No. of Skeins

Yarn Inventory

Name:	Dye lot:	Source:	No. of Skeins

Yarn Inventory

Name:	Dye lot:	Source:	No. of Skeins

Yarn Inventory

Name:	Dye lot:	Source:	No. of Skeins

Yarn Inventory

Name:	Dye lot:	Source:	No. of Skeins

Needle Inventory

Size:	Type:	Length:	Source:

Needle Inventory

Size:	Type:	Length:	Source:

Common Abbreviations in Patterns

approx	approximately
beg	begin, beginning
BO	bind off
ch	chain
cm(s)	centimeter(s)
cn	cable needle
CO	cast on
cont	continue, continuing
dec	decrease, decreasing
dpns	double-pointed needles
foll	following
g	grams
inc	increase, increasing
k	knit
k1B or k1-tbl	knit 1 stitch through back loop
k2tog	knit 2 stitches together
k2tog-tbl OR k2tog-b	knit 2 stitches together through back loop
k-inc or KFB	inc 1 by knitting into the front and back loops of next st
LH	left-hand
lp(s)	loop(s)
m1	make 1 st knitwise; single knit increase
M1-L	make 1 st by knitting into the LEFT strand of the st 2 rows below the st just knit
M1-R	make 1 st by knitting into the RIGHT strand of the st 1 row below the next st
m	meters
MC	main color
mult	multiple
oz(s)	ounces
p	purl
p1-b or p-tbl	purl 1 stitch through back loop
p2tog	purl 2 stitches together
p2tog tbl OR p2tog-b	purl 2 stitches together through back loop
patt or pat	pattern

Common Abbreviations in Patterns

pm	place marker
psso	pass slipped stitch over
rem	remains, remaining
rep	repeat
RH	right-hand
RS	right side
rnd	round
sk	skip
SKP	slip 1, knit 1, pass slip stitch over
SK2P	slip 1, knit 2 together, pass slip stitch over the knit 2 together
sl	slip
sl1k	slip 1 stitch knitwise
sl1p	dslip 1 stitch purlwise
sl st	slip stitch
sm	slip marker
ssk	slip 2 stitches knitwise, return to left needle and knit together through back loops
ssp	slip 2 stitches knitwise, return to left needle and purltogether through back loops
st(s)	stitch(es)
tbl	through back loop
tfl	through front loop
tog	together
W&T	wrap and turn (for working short rows)
WS	wrong side
wyib	with yarn in back
wyif	with yarn in front
yb	yarn back
yf	yarn forward
yd(s)	yards
yo	yarn over
yrn	yarn round needle
*	repeat instructions following * as many times as necessary or until the end of the row
[ ]	repeat instructions within brackets as many times as indicated

Made in the USA
Columbia, SC
29 June 2020